SKATEBOARDING

Andy Horsley

 Crabtree Publishing Company

www.crabtreebooks.com

Crabtree Publishing Company

www.crabtreebooks.com   1-800-387-7650

Author: Andy Horsley
Project editor: Ruth Owen
Project designer: Sara Greasley
Photo research: Lizzie Knowles
Proofreaders: Robert Walker,
   Crystal Sikkens
Production coordinator:
   Katherine Kantor
Prepress technician:
   Katherine Kantor

With thanks to series editors Honor Head and Jean Coppendale.

Thank you to Lorraine Petersen and the members of nasen

**Published
in Canada
Crabtree Publishing**
616 Welland Ave.
St. Catharines, ON
L2M 5V6

**Published in the
United States
Crabtree Publishing**
PMB16A
350 Fifth Ave., Suite 3308
New York, NY 10118

Content development by Shakespeare Squared
www.ShakespeareSquared.com
First published in Great Britain in 2008 by ticktock Media Ltd,
2 Orchard Business Centre, North Farm Road,
Tunbridge Wells, Kent, TN2 3XF
Copyright © ticktock Entertainment Ltd 2008

Picture credits:
Alamy: Ben Molyneux: p. 10;
   Wig Worland: p. 29
Andrew Horsley: p. 1, 7, 12–13, 15,
   16, 17, 18–19, 20, 21, 22, 23, 24,
   25, 26, 27, 28
Getty Images: Christian Petersen: p. 8–9
Pixland: Jupiter Images: p. 9
Rex Features: Everett Collection: p. 6 (bottom)
Shutterstock: cover, p. 2, 4–5, 8, 11, 14

Library and Archives Canada Cataloguing in Publication

Horsley, Andy
      Skateboarding / Andy Horsley.

(Crabtree contact)
Includes index.
ISBN 978-0-7787-3771-1 (bound).--ISBN 978-0-7787-3793-3
(pbk.)

      1. Skateboarding--Juvenile literature. I. Title. II. Series.

GV859.8.H675 2008   j796.22   C2008-903498-8

Library of Congress Cataloging-in-Publication Data

Horsley, Andy, 1972-
   Skateboarding / Andy Horsley.
      p. cm. -- (Crabtree contact)
   Includes index.
   ISBN-13: 978-0-7787-3793-3 (pbk. : alk. paper)
   ISBN-10: 0-7787-3793-4 (pbk. : alk. paper)
   ISBN-13: 978-0-7787-3771-1 (reinforced library binding : alk. paper)
   ISBN-10: 0-7787-3771-3 (reinforced library binding : alk. paper)
   1. Skateboarding--Juvenile literature. I. Title. II. Series.

GV859.8.H68 2009
796.22--dc22

                                                        2008023539

CONTENTS

WARNING!

The tricks featured in this book have been performed by experienced skateboarders. Neither the publisher nor the author shall be liable for any bodily harm or damage to property that may happen as a result of trying the tricks in this book. In many places, it is illegal to skateboard. Look out for signs. Do not break the law.

NO SKATEBOARDING

...a secret world!

Skateboarding has its own language. It has its own heroes. It also has its own style of clothing.

Skateboarding will change the way that you look at the streets.

Welcome to the **underground** world of skateboarding.

"I love skateboarding. It helps me be me. It's how I feel free."

Skateboarder Rodney Mullen: he invented the kickflip by accident — he was trying an **ollie**.

5

Skateboarding was invented in the late 1960s in the United States.

Surfers began skateboarding when waves were not big enough to ride. They **carved** up the streets of California. Soon, the number of skateboarders grew.

Skateboarding was shown in the 1970s TV show *Wonder Woman*. Today's skateboards are more narrow than the boards used in the 1970s.

The ollie is the most important trick to learn.
It was invented by Alan "Ollie" Gelfand in 1977.
You need to ollie to be able to do most tricks.

The ollie helps you get
the board off the ground.

OLLIE

To do an ollie, first kick down on the
tail of the board. At the same time,
drag your front foot up the **griptape**.
As you do this, you must jump, as well.

Today, people skateboard all over the world.

Some skateboarders are **professional**. Professional skaters earn money by skateboarding. They skate in competitions and events to promote skateboarding.

Skateboarding appears in magazines, music videos, and video games.

"I felt like I'd made it when I appeared in a video game."
Paul Rodriguez, street skater

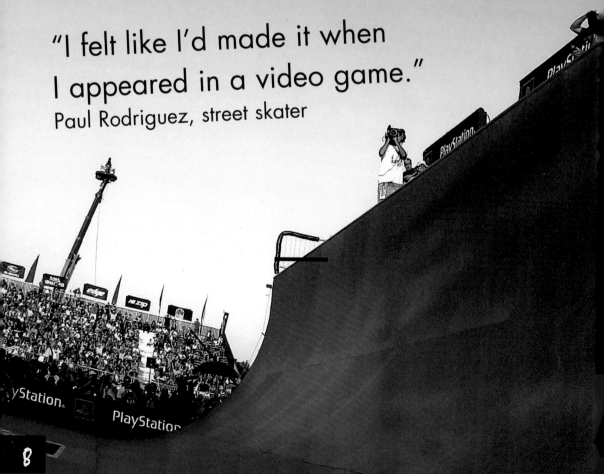

Anything goes in skateboarding fashion. Skaters wear baggy jeans, tight jeans, sweatpants, or shorts. There are thousands of shoe designs to choose from, too.

Skateboarding was one of the original sports included in the **X Games**. The X Games is the world's largest **extreme sports** competition. Each year, the best skaters compete in this event.

The **graphics** on skateboard decks often express a skater's personal style.

You can buy a deck from a store with graphics you like or design your deck using paint or stickers to make it **unique**.

The top of the skateboard deck is covered with griptape. Griptape is rough like sandpaper. It helps the rider's feet grip the deck.

Trucks attach the wheels to the deck. Trucks help you make turns.

Wheel

STREET STYLE

Many people start ripping up the streets when they first discover skateboarding. They use **street furniture** to do tricks.

Street decks are thin
and small, with small,
light wheels.

PARK LIFE

Many cities have **skateparks** with **half-pipes**, **bowls**, and other **obstacles**.

Skateboarders use the obstacles to perform flips, spins, and grabs high in the air.

HALF-PIPE

Skateparks are ideal places to meet with friends. You can show off your new tricks. You can also see local heroes **killing it** on the obstacles.

BOWL

SKATESPEAK

Dinosaur parks — Old, concrete skateparks that were built in the 1970s.
Mini-ramp — A small halfpipe about 5 feet (1.5 meter) high.

RAMP IT UP!

A **vert ramp** is a big halfpipe about 11.5 feet (3.5 meters) high. Helmets and pads are a must for this type of skateboarding.

VERT RAMP

Vert ramps are where skateboarders learn to fly!

Shorts allow the skater to wear knee pads.

Helmet

Elbow pads

Big wheels gain more speed. They also help the skater land big tricks.

Vert decks are wider than street decks. Wider decks give better control and **stability**.

DEMOS AND COMPS

Skateboard competitions are held all over the world.

You will get to see skateboard superstars and top skateboard team **demos**.

At the end of a demo, the teams give out free stickers, t-shirts, and even decks!

So make sure you stay until the end!

The vert section of a vert ramp is vertical — it goes straight up!

FROM THE GROUND UP

Beginner skateboarders are called grommets.

To become a great skateboarder, you will need to learn some basic tricks, such as ollies, flips, and grinds.

KICKFLIP

A kickflip is when the board spins 360 degrees around its length underneath you. After it has spun, you need to land back on the board.

GRIND

To perform a grind, you must slide your trucks across the rail. Grinding both trucks at once is called a 50-50 grind.

SKATESPEAK

Fakie – travelling backward
Gnarly – dangerous or extreme
Goofy – standing right foot forward
Rad – super good
Regular – standing with left foot forward
Ripping – skateboarding very well
Sick – good
Slam – when you fall off your board

FLIPS

There are many types of flips to keep you kicking and spinning. Here are some difficult ones.

360 FLIP

The board spins 360 degrees and flips at the same time.

BACKSIDE FLIP

The board flips and turns 180 degrees. You follow the board and ride away backward.

FAKIE KICKFLIP

This is a kickflip going backward.

GRIND ON

The trucks of your deck can be used to grind along edges and rails.

It's a tricky combo of power and balance.

NOSE GRIND

A nose grind is when you rub just the front truck on a rail.

FEEBLE GRIND

A **feeble grind** is a tough trick. You need to jump the front truck over the rail. At the same time, you need to grind on the back truck.

YOUR DOMAIN

The streets and skateparks where you live are now your **domain**.

It's time to explore!

WALLRIDE TO FAKIE

Ramps will allow you to get the air you need to perform tricks.

KICKFLIP

Stairs are no longer used just to walk up and down. You can kickflip them!

50-50 GRINDS

Railings become train tracks for 50–50 grinds.

If you learn some good tricks and perform them well, you can film them. Then you can make a "sponsor me" tape.

Send the tape to your favorite skateboard company. If they like your moves, they might send you free stuff, such as brand new skateboards and t-shirts.

Professional skateboarders get paid to skate! Their **sponsorship** company sends the skater all over the world to enter competitions.

Tony Hawk

Top pro Tony Hawk has his own movie company, computer game, and a brand of clothing.

NEED-TO-KNOW WORDS

carve To turn sharply on your board

demo A skateboard team showing off their moves

domain Your area — the places you skate most often

extreme sports Exciting and potentially dangerous sports

graphics The pictures or designs on the underside of the deck

griptape A material on the board that helps skateboarders control it

killing it Skatespeak for skating at a very high standard

obstacles Halfpipes, ramps, stairs — anything that you can skateboard on

ollie A skateboard jump. The ollie is the best way to get all four wheels off the ground

skateparks Indoor or outdoor parks designed for skateboarding. Skateparks have many obstacles on which skaters can practice tricks

sponsorship When a company gives a skateboarder free stuff, such as decks. If you are really good, a company may pay you to skate for them and advertise their products

stability Making something steady so it is not wobbly

surfer Rides on waves using a board

trucks The metal parts that fix the wheels to the deck

underground To be alternative and outside the mainstream

unique The only one of its kind

X Games A series of extreme sports competitions sponsored by ESPN. The X Games includes events such as BMX, surfing, and motocross